DAYS OF CHANGE

Creative Education

BY VALERIE BODDEN

Published by Creative Education
P.O. Box 227, Mankato, Minnesota 56002
Creative Education is an imprint of The Creative Company.

Cover design and art direction by Rita Marshall
Interior design and book production by The Design Lab
Printed in the United States of America

Photographs by Alamy (Roger Hutchings, Keith Lewis),
Corbis (Diane Bondareff, Rupert Stephane), Getty Images
(AFP, Time Life Pictures)

Library of Congress Cataloging-in-Publication Data
Bodden, Valerie.
The 9/11 terror attacks / by Valerie Bodden.
p. cm. – (Days of change)
Includes bibliographical references and index.
ISBN-13: 978-1-58341-549-8
1. September 11 Terrorist Attacks, 2001. I. Title.
HV6432.7.B57 2006
973.931–dc22   2006020542

First edition
9 8 7 6 5 4 3 2 1

CORNING PUBLIC LIBRARY
603 9th Street
Corning, Iowa 50841

THE 9/11 TERROR ATTACKS

On September 11, pedestrians watched in horror as the World Trade Center towers—then the most dominant features of the famous New York City skyline—burned and collapsed.

Usually unfazed by the out-of-the-ordinary,

many New Yorkers looked up on the morning of September 11, 2001, as a low rumble reverberated through Manhattan. Several raised their heads just in time to witness a passenger jet slamming into the tallest building in a city of towering structures, the north tower of the World Trade Center. An angry fireball roared from the tower's 93rd to 99th floors as onlookers saw aircraft pieces, desks, and even gruesome body parts rain from the building. No one yet knew that the tower had just become the first target in a massive terrorist attack. Soon, planes would crash into the World Trade Center's south tower, the Pentagon, and a farmer's field in Pennsylvania, shocking the world and bringing Americans together in a newfound spirit of unity.

Yet, even as Americans drew together to support their country, many questioned why the government had been unable to prevent the attacks, which were quickly attributed to Islamic terrorists long known for their hatred of the United States. A Congressional commission was established to investigate the attacks, and the U.S. launched a global war on terror. At the same time, Americans tried to return to their everyday lives, knowing now that their country wasn't invincible and fearing that more attacks were inevitable.

5

September 11, 2001

As the calendar turned from December 1999 to January 2000, marking the beginning of the 21st century, the world was a much smaller place than it had been 100 years before. Although countries were still as far apart geographically as ever, the dawn of the digital age had given people the ability to communicate instantaneously with others half a world away via e-mail, instant messaging using the Internet, television, satellite radio, and cell phones. A global transportation network of high-speed jets enabled people to travel from country to country with ease, and global trade meant that the products purchased in one region of the world had often been produced in another.

In the U.S., global trade and communication had become a taken-for-granted part of everyday life, as people around the country purchased items manufactured overseas on a daily basis. Americans had also fully embraced technology by the end of the 20th century, and computers and other digital devices were being used to control everything from utility systems and traffic signals to bank records and medical equipment. In fact, the greatest concern in the U.S. as the millennium approached was that computers might not be programmed to handle the change in date from 1999 to 2000 and would malfunction, causing a breakdown in vital services. When the first New Year's Day of the new millennium passed without a hitch, many people breathed easier.

Not all areas of American life depended on technology, however.

A SMALL WORLD

6

In order to attract people to their cause, Islamic extremists have twisted parts of the Koran to suit their purposes. They claim that the Koran's references to *jihad*, which literally means "struggle," describe a struggle against infidels. However, most of the world's one and a quarter billion Muslims believe that jihad refers to a struggle with oneself to become a better Muslim. In addition, although the Koran forbids suicide, stating that those who commit suicide will have to endlessly repeat the manner of their deaths, extremists lure suicide bombers with the promise of a painless death and a direct path to heaven.

All Muslims hold the Koran in high regard, but extremists and militants interpret the holy book differently than do mainstream believers, many of whom live in the U.S.

In many regions of the country, electronic voting systems had not yet replaced old-fashioned punch-card ballots for elections, a fact that caused many problems in the 2000 presidential election, which proved to be the closest in U.S. history. A dispute over the votes in the state of Florida meant that for more than a month after the November election, Americans were unsure whether Texas governor George W. Bush or Vice President Al Gore would be the next president. Finally, after the Supreme Court weighed in, Bush was declared the winner. When the new president entered office in January 2001, he found himself at the helm of the world's sole superpower, a nation with a superior military and the leading position in world trade.

Meanwhile, to the south of America, Mexican elections were also making news in 2000, as Vicente Fox was elected president in July—the first time in 71 years that the country's corrupt Institutional Revolutionary Party had been defeated. Farther south, in Colombia, the government was engaged in a long-standing war against guerilla fighters seeking to set up a socialist state, while at the same time struggling to bring the country's flourishing drug trade under control with a new program designed to kill off the coca plant, from which cocaine is made.

"I feel this way about it. World trade means world peace, and consequently the World Trade Center buildings in New York . . . had a bigger purpose than just to provide room for tenants. The World Trade Center is a living symbol of man's dedication to world peace. . . . Beyond the compelling need to make this a monument to world peace, the World Trade Center should, because of its importance, become a representation of man's belief in humanity, his need for individual dignity, his beliefs in the cooperation of men, and through cooperation, his ability to find greatness."

MINORU YAMASAKI, World Trade Center architect, 1970s

8

Across the Atlantic, the countries of the European Union—a confederation of European nations—had become an economic power second only to the U.S. in the production of goods and services, and most citizens enjoyed a relatively high standard of living. Not all of Europe experienced stability at the start of the 21st century, however. In eastern Europe, civil war throughout the 1990s had torn apart the Balkan states of Croatia, Bosnia, and the region of Kosovo in Serbia, and a brutal policy of "ethnic cleansing" aimed at killing or expelling non-Serbs from the area had resulted in the flight of huge numbers of refugees. Although a peace plan was finally signed in 1999, conditions were slow to improve, as millions of citizens had been displaced during the course of the decade.

In 1993, Croat forces attacked the Bosnian village of Ahmici, destroying many homes, damaging the village's two mosques, and killing an estimated 116 Muslims.

Instability also rocked Russia during the last years of the 20th century, and many citizens found themselves worse off than they had been under the communist Soviet Union, which had been dissolved in 1991. Widespread unemployment left many without the means to support their families, and crime ruled the streets, as the Russian mafia took advantage of the government's weakness. In the southwestern region of the country known as Chechnya, war raged as rebels attempted to secede from Russia and create an independent Islamic state. In March 2000, Vladimir Putin became the country's second democratically elected president, promising to strengthen the government and boost the nation's standard of living.

Meanwhile, in China, the world's only remaining communist power after the fall of the Soviet Union, a growing middle class began to enjoy modest luxuries in the 1990s, such as private homes, cars, and cell phones, for the first time. Yet citizens were still subject to restrictions on political speech, and human rights violations were commonplace. In North Korea, too, people faced severe limits on free speech, and those who dared to speak out against Kim Jong Il and his government were often imprisoned in detention camps, where many were tortured or murdered.

At the same time, in Africa, many citizens suffered from the effects of unemployment, disease—including AIDS, which had

Throughout the 1990s, Russian troops (above) and Chechen rebels were locked in fierce battle, resulting in the deaths of more than 46,000 people, most of them civilians.

"It is far better for anyone to kill a single American soldier than to squander his efforts on other activities. . . . We believe that the worst thieves in the world today and the worst terrorists are the Americans. . . . We do not have to differentiate between military or civilian. As far as we are concerned, they are all targets."

OSAMA BIN LADEN,
Al Qaeda leader,
May 1998

Al Qaeda leader Osama bin Laden

reached epidemic proportions on the continent—and war. African nations such as the Congo, Algeria, and Sierra Leone were torn apart by conflict during the last years of the 20th century. In the Middle East, violence continued to rock Israel and Palestine, and the peace process between the two nations—at odds since the formation of Israel as a Jewish homeland on formerly Palestinian territory in 1948—had come to a standstill, although the U.S. continued its attempts to facilitate a peace agreement.

Just outside the Middle East, in Afghanistan, war raged between the country's Taliban government and its main opposition group, the Northern Alliance. The Taliban had taken power in the mid-1990s, imposing a strict Muslim regime that outlawed televisions, non-religious music, dancing, movies, paintings, photography, and even chessboards, and required women to keep their heads and bodies covered.

The Taliban's fundamentalist, or strict, interpretation of the Koran, the holy book of the Islamic religion, made the country a natural refuge for Osama bin Laden, a wealthy Muslim fundamentalist who headed a well-organized international terrorist network known as Al Qaeda (Arabic for "the base"). With terrorist training camps in Afghanistan

15

Some Muslims, such as these youths in Pakistan, voiced a hatred for the U.S. before September 11, burning flags to protest American influence in the Arab world.

and several thousand members spread throughout more than 50 countries, Al Qaeda aimed to incite jihad, or holy war, to overthrow the governments of Muslim countries that didn't rule by what it considered true Islamic principles, as well as to fight the presence of "infidels"—those who don't believe in Islam—in Muslim lands.

For years, bin Laden had called the U.S. the chief infidel—the "Great Satan"—because of its influence in the Middle East, including its perceived favoritism of Israel in the peace process between Israel and Palestine. Bin Laden was also angered by the presence of American troops in Middle Eastern countries—especially Saudi Arabia, home to some of Islam's holiest sites—as he believed that their presence defiled the land. Thus, in 1996, bin Laden had declared jihad against Americans, claiming that every Muslim had the duty to push "the American enemy out of the holy land." In 1998, bin Laden had gone even farther, calling on Muslims to attack Americans anywhere in the world.

Although many in the West (the part of the world including the U.S. and Europe) knew that the U.S. was Al Qaeda's primary target—Al Qaeda attacks against U.S. embassies in Kenya and Tanzania in 1998 and against the

"God Almighty . . . has prohibited injustice among humans. Aggression against those who have committed no crime and the killing of innocent people . . . are not permissible even during wars and invasions. Killing the weak, infants, women, and the elderly, and destroying property, are considered serious crimes in Islam. Acts of corruption and even laying waste to the land are forbidden by God and His Prophet. . . . Those who commit such crimes are the worst of people. Anyone who thinks that any Islamic scholar will condone such acts is totally wrong."

SALIH BIN MUHAMMAD AL-LUHEIDAN, chairman of the Supreme Judicial Council of Saudi Arabia, September 14, 2001

16

Osama bin Laden has not always been a Muslim fundamentalist. Born in 1957 to a wealthy Saudi Arabian family, bin Laden was a devout, though not fanatical, Muslim as a boy. At the age of 11, he inherited a huge fortune—some estimates run as high as $300 million—from his father. The course of bin Laden's life changed forever when, while studying engineering at King Abdul Aziz University in Saudi Arabia, he enrolled in an Islamic studies course taught by a professor who encouraged the establishment of completely Muslim nations, governed by Islamic law. From that time on, bin Laden dedicated his life—and his money—to the cause.

Osama bin Laden boasts thousands of supporters—both young and old—around the world; many of them are not formally aligned with Al Qaeda but support its aims.

As unlikely as it may seem, the United States was once allied with the group that later formed the core of Al Qaeda. When the Soviet Union invaded Afghanistan in the 1980s, the U.S., determined to prevent Soviet communist influence from taking hold in the country, aligned itself with Afghan resistance fighters called the *mujahedeen*, who were funded in part by Osama bin Laden. When the mujahedeen eventually drove the Soviets from their country, the U.S. immediately withdrew all support for the fighters, angering many of them, who soon joined bin Laden's new terror network: Al Qaeda.

In October 2000, Al Qaeda suicide bombers exploded a small boat next to the USS *Cole*, ripping a large hole into the vessel's hull and killing 17 U.S. sailors.

navy destroyer USS *Cole* in 2000 had proven so—most Americans didn't worry about terrorism as they went about their daily lives, and when the subject did come up, rarely did anyone consider the possibility of attacks on American soil. What few realized, however, was that during 2000 and 2001, Al Qaeda-trained terrorists had been quietly entering the country, doing everything possible—shaving their beards, uncovering their heads, carrying cigarettes—to blend in with their neighbors. All the while, these men were waiting patiently for their orders from Al Qaeda. Those orders would soon unleash terror in the most powerful nation on Earth.

It was business as usual inside the twin towers of the World Trade Center on the morning of Tuesday, September 11, 2001. Literally thousands of people were passing through the buildings' doors, headed for offices on one of the 110 floors of either building. Most of them worked at investment banks or brokerage houses, such as Cantor Fitzgerald or Euro Brokers, while others worked for the Windows on the World restaurant, located on the 106th and 107th floors of the north tower, or the Port Authority, the buildings' independent police force.

By 8:46 A.M. that morning, more than 16,000 of the 50,000 people who worked in the towers had arrived. As they began to settle into their routines—pouring coffee, checking e-mail, answering phone calls—there was suddenly a huge explosion inside the north tower. People above and below the site of the explosion looked at each other in shock. Some wandered around their offices, searching for someone who could tell them what had happened; others called the building's information desk, asking what to do next. Most had no idea that American Airlines Flight 11, carrying 92 people, had just crashed into the building, ripping through the 93rd through 99th floors, its more than 10,000 gallons (37,850 l) of jet fuel exploding and setting off a raging fire.

While those on the floors above and below the crash tried to figure out what was going on, the few who had survived the impact on the floors nearest the crash desperately looked for a way out. Some fought through

ATTACK ON AMERICA

20

After the north tower of the World Trade Center was hit, many in the south tower debated whether or not to evacuate. The Port Authority, seeking to avoid the chaos of a mass evacuation, urged people to stay where they were. Even in the north tower, a mass evacuation was not ordered immediately, as the policy for high-rise buildings had long been to evacuate only the floors impacted by fire, as well as the floor directly above them, since these floors were supposed to be able to contain the fire. Unfortunately, such a policy did not take into account the possibility of the building's collapse.

Although complete evacuation of the World Trade Center didn't begin immediately after the attack, the majority of those below the impact zone in each tower managed to escape.

the debris and blinding smoke to search for one of the building's three stairways. Others, trapped in their offices by devouring flames, retreated to the windows, leaning out as far as they could. Some hung from the windows until their grip gave out and they fell; others, with no hope of escaping the torture of being burned alive, jumped to their deaths.

Outside, hundreds of firefighters and police officers raced to the site, along with television news crews from around the city. Within minutes, live images of the roaring fire were being broadcast across the nation and around the world. Many news anchors were at a loss to explain what had happened; most believed that the crash had been a terrible accident. Just minutes later, they would learn otherwise.

At 9:03 A.M., as news cameras remained trained on the north tower

Thousands of firefighters and police officers responded to the emergency at the World Trade Center on the morning of September 11. Confident that the buildings would remain standing as they had after a bomb had been detonated in the underground garage of the towers in 1993 (also an attack by Islamic extremists), department chiefs set up command posts in the towers' lobbies. When the towers collapsed, hundreds of officers and firefighters were still in the buildings. All told, the events of September 11 cost the lives of 343 New York City firefighters—the largest number of fatalities ever experienced by an emergency response agency—and 60 police officers.

More than a third of New York's fire companies were dispatched to the World Trade Center on September 11; many found themselves overwhelmed by the events of the day.

American Airlines Flight 77 hit the Pentagon at an angle, so the damage was worse on the inside than it appeared on the outside, affecting three of the building's five rings.

of the World Trade Center, United Airlines Flight 175, carrying 65 people, suddenly entered the frame, banked, and slammed into the south tower. Once again, a powerful explosion rocked the area as flames burst from the impact site at the 77th through 85th floors, slightly lower than that on the north tower. As people across the globe watched the unbelievable scene on their televisions, they suddenly realized that America was under attack.

More than 230 miles (370 km) away, news of the attack had reached military officials at the Pentagon in Arlington, Virginia, a suburb of Washington, D.C. Despite the fact that the Pentagon, which houses the U.S. Department of Defense, was thought to be one of the safest buildings in the world—with 24-inch-thick (61 cm) walls of limestone, brick, and concrete—many of the 23,000 people who worked there were on edge. Some feared that their enormous five-sided building would be the next target.

"The threat of terrorism has always been, for most Americans, an abstraction. But that changed with Tuesday's [September 11, 2001] spectacular televised attack. The toll went far beyond the thousands of lost lives and the destruction of the preeminent symbol of the New York skyline. Our sense of security and much of our innocence was lost as well."

BOB HERBERT, *New York Times* columnist, September 13, 2001

25

Their fears were soon justified. At 9:37 A.M., American Airlines Flight 77—with 64 people aboard—slammed into the Pentagon at 530 miles (850 km) per hour and exploded. Fortunately, the area of the building where the plane struck had recently been renovated with blast-resistant windows, fire sprinklers, and steel columns. Although these additions reduced the plane's impact, the destruction inside the building was still massive. As those inside feverishly searched for survivors in the impact area, another drama was unfolding in the air above Pennsylvania.

Earlier that morning, 37 passengers and 7 crew members had boarded United Flight 93 in Newark, New Jersey, bound for San Francisco. Forty-six minutes into the flight, four men who had been riding in first class stood up and stormed the cockpit, taking over the plane's controls. Wielding box cutters and claiming to have a bomb, they forced the passengers to the back of the plane, where one terrorist stood guard, seemingly unconcerned that several passengers were beginning to call home on cell phones and the plane's air phones. As their family members told them

The FBI credits the passengers and crew members of all four hijacked airplanes with helping them to determine the identities of the hijackers. Before each plane crashed, at least one person onboard used a cell phone or air phone to call a family member or the authorities to report the plane's hijacking. Using the callers' descriptions of the hijackers and their seat numbers, the FBI was able to quickly identify exactly who had carried out each attack. Air traffic control transmissions from the airplanes, as well as the voice recorder from Flight 93, helped authorities further piece together what had happened.

The September 11 attacks were immediately compared to the infamous 1941 Pearl Harbor bombing; "extra" editions dedicated solely to the tragedy were printed worldwide.

"To those who say that our city will never be the same, I say you are right. It will be better. Now we understand much more clearly why people from all over the globe want to come to New York, and to America . . . why they always have, and why they always will. It's called freedom, equal protection under law, respect for human life, and the promise of opportunity."

RUDOLPH GIULIANI, New York City mayor at the time of the September 11 attacks, September 23, 2001

what had happened in New York and Washington, D.C., the passengers realized the awful truth—they were about to become the fourth weapon in a new kind of terrorist attack.

Quickly, the passengers formulated a plan to rush the hijackers and take back the plane. Together, several of them raced to the cockpit, where they struggled against the hijackers for five minutes before the plane crashed in a field outside Shanksville, Pennsylvania, at 10:02 A.M., killing everyone aboard but preventing the hijackers from hitting their ultimate target, most likely the White House or the Capitol building in Washington, D.C.

As the passengers on Flight 93 struggled for their lives, those who had survived the impacts at the World Trade Center were, for the most part, calmly filing down the stairways in each tower, helping those who were

Rescue workers carefully steered people exiting the World Trade Center away from falling debris.

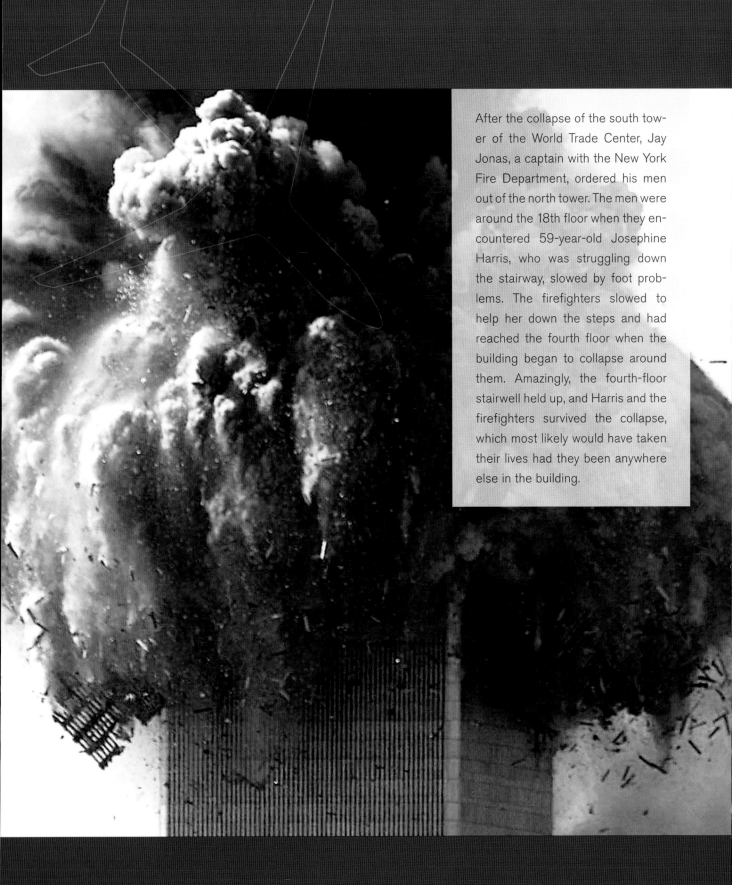

After the collapse of the south tower of the World Trade Center, Jay Jonas, a captain with the New York Fire Department, ordered his men out of the north tower. The men were around the 18th floor when they encountered 59-year-old Josephine Harris, who was struggling down the stairway, slowed by foot problems. The firefighters slowed to help her down the steps and had reached the fourth floor when the building began to collapse around them. Amazingly, the fourth-floor stairwell held up, and Harris and the firefighters survived the collapse, which most likely would have taken their lives had they been anywhere else in the building.

As the World Trade Center towers collapsed, the ground shook and huge chunks of debris—some the size of houses—careened toward the ground.

disabled and stepping aside to let the injured pass. As workers were streaming out of the buildings, firefighters were entering, each lugging more than 60 pounds (27 kg) of oxygen tanks and hoses up toward the sites of the impacts, where huge fires continued to blaze.

The fires were doing more than devouring office furniture and memos, however. They were generating enough heat—up to 2,000 °F (1,090 °C)—to weaken the buildings' steel structures. At 9:59 A.M., the south tower suddenly collapsed, one floor crashing down onto the next until the entire building was gone. People in the street first stood transfixed at the sight, then, realizing that an enormous cloud of debris was headed straight for them, ran for their lives, ducking into buildings as the choking cloud overtook them. Dust covered everyone and everything for blocks, shutting out the sunlight and leaving many people in total darkness. When the dust cleared enough for people to see, only one tower remained standing.

"Then the building [north tower of the World Trade Center] starts to collapse. It is an incredible sound, like the combination of an oncoming locomotive and an avalanche, with a huge windstorm right behind. Everything is shaking, like in an earthquake, and it feels like an eternity, that it is never going to stop. . . . But now there is a dead silence."

DAVE LIM, Port Authority police officer, 2002

31

For another 29 minutes, the north tower stood, minus its twin. Then, at 10:28, it too collapsed, causing the same chaotic dash for cover and the same blinding, choking cloud of debris. This time, when the dust cleared, nothing but a nine-story pile of rubble remained where once had stood two of America's grandest buildings. Fires burned throughout the devastation, and a thick layer of ash and soot covered the streets of Manhattan. Rescue crews immediately began digging through the rubble, searching for survivors but finding few.

Even as all of these events were still unfolding, the U.S. government had sprung into action. By the time the south tower fell, all planes in the country had been ordered to land—the first such order in the nation's history—and incoming international flights had been diverted to Canada. Fighter planes were ordered to protect New York and Washington, D.C., and warships and aircraft carriers took up positions near the cities. That evening, President Bush appeared on television and promised broad retribution against the terrorists, saying that no distinction would be made between those who had committed the attacks and the nations that harbored them.

All around the world, people grieved with the U.S. World leaders called to express their condolences, and a French newspaper printed the headline *Nous sommes tous Américains* ("We are all Americans"). Even as most of the world supported the U.S., however, some Muslim fundamentalists living in Palestinian areas of Israel celebrated the victory of Islamic terrorists against the West. This "victory" had claimed the lives of almost 3,000 people.

On September 11, ordinary people became heroes, giving their lives to save others. In the north tower of the World Trade Center, one man in particular helped to save life after life. After first scouting the 88th floor to help his coworkers find a safe way down, Port Authority officer Frank De Martini went up a floor and, with the help of others, freed a group of people trapped behind a door. He and his group then searched the surrounding floors for people in need of assistance. Based on the accounts of survivors, it is likely that De Martini helped to save at least 70 people. He was killed when the tower collapsed.

As rescue workers searched for survivors amid the tangled ruins of the World Trade Center, they had to watch out for hot spots and loose debris that could cause a cave-in.

In the days that followed the attacks, Americans from around the country flooded New York, Washington, D.C., and Pennsylvania with cards, flowers, and other memorials. Donations of money—a total of $1.4 billion—and needed items poured in to the charities assisting the victims of the attacks, and volunteers from around the world arrived to offer their assistance.

In New York, light posts became missing-persons billboards as family members searched for news of their missing loved ones, hoping against hope that they hadn't been killed in the towers' collapse. Rescue efforts continued at a fever pitch at the site of the World Trade Center rubble, which came to be known as Ground Zero. Ultimately, only a handful of survivors were found at the World Trade Center site, the last

NEVER FORGET

on September 12. But for days after the attacks, operations continued to be referred to as a "rescue mission." (At the Pentagon, too, rescue teams continued to work, spending nearly two weeks searching for survivors— but finding none after the first day.)

Finally, two weeks after the attacks, the rescue mission at Ground Zero shifted to a recovery operation, and cleanup of the site began. Twenty-four hours a day, 7 days a week, up to 700 people and 500 huge machines and trucks worked at the site, dismantling the ruins piece by piece and taking them to a nearby landfill, where the debris was examined for evidence. Whenever workers at Ground Zero located a body, all work at the site was stopped until it was removed, a final attempt to honor those who had lost their lives

In addition to hanging photos of the missing around the city, many New Yorkers filled out lengthy forms describing their loved ones to aid in identifying the dead.

When the World Trade Center towers fell, they caused enormous damage to surrounding buildings, many of which later had to be razed to the ground.

in the horrific attack. It took eight and a half months to haul away the site's two million tons (1.8 million t) of debris, at a cost of $600 million.

While mourning the loss of life and cleaning up the devastation, Americans also focused on finding out who had been responsible for the attacks. By the afternoon of September 11, the FBI had set up a command center for a full-scale investigation that would come to involve more than 7,000 agents. Before the week was out, the FBI had learned the identities of all of the hijackers— 19 in total—of the four planes. They soon also learned that several of the hijackers had taken flight lessons in the U.S. and that almost all of them had connections to one man: Osama bin Laden.

Knowing that bin Laden had taken refuge in Afghanistan, President Bush ordered the Taliban to turn the

After September 11, newspapers printed "wanted" posters for Osama bin Laden, and the U.S. government offered a $25 million reward for information leading to his capture.

terrorist leader over. The Taliban refused, and on October 7, 2001, the U.S. began bombing Afghanistan, the first target in its new "war on terror." By the end of November, American troops and Afghanistan's Northern Alliance had driven the Taliban from power, although they were unable to capture bin Laden. For the first time in years, Afghanis listened to music and watched television, and women walked through the streets with their faces uncovered.

At home, life had changed for Americans as well. After the attacks, many people were fearful, not knowing when or where terrorists might strike again. In the days after September 11, bomb scares in New York led to the evacuation of several transportation centers, including Grand Central Terminal and LaGuardia Airport. Fears of another attack seemed justified when, just a

Although Al Qaeda members worked hard to blend in with everyday Americans, Al Qaeda operative Zacarias Moussaoui raised the suspicions of a flight school owner in Minnesota when he expressed an interest in learning only to steer a jet in midair. The flight school owner called the FBI, and Moussaoui was arrested in August 2001 on immigration charges. After the September 11 attack, it was discovered that Moussaoui had information that may have helped authorities uncover the terrorist plot before it was carried out. Moussaoui subsequently pled guilty to charges of conspiracy in connection with the attacks and in 2006 was sentenced to life in prison without the possibility of parole.

After the U.S. invaded Afghanistan, many Al Qaeda members hid in mountain caves but were apprehended by anti-Taliban fighters (with rifle) aided by U.S. forces.

Two of the people killed in the anthrax attacks after September 11 were postal workers; as a result, many postal workers began to wear protective gloves when handling the mail.

week after September 11, letters containing deadly anthrax bacteria began to show up at media and government offices in Florida, New York, and Washington, D.C., killing five people in what remains an unsolved crime.

Besides having a new fear of their mail, many Americans were suddenly reluctant to fly. When people did begin returning to the nation's airports, they found themselves facing long security lines and a new list of restrictions for carry-on items. A new law required an increased number of undercover federal air marshals on flights, especially those considered to be at high risk of hijacking. Despite the new security measures, tensions aboard planes were high, and several flights were canceled or diverted because of security threats.

In spite of—or perhaps because of—their fears, people across America, and in New York especially, were suddenly nicer to one another. They applauded police officers and firefighters. Stores everywhere sold out of American flags, and military recruitment offices noticed a spike in inquiries. Even in the political arena, an unprecedented sense of cooperation characterized relations between Democrats and Republicans, who worked

"A terrorist attack designed to tear us apart has instead bound us together as a nation. . . . In the past week, we have seen the American people at their very best everywhere in America. Citizens have come together to pray, to give blood, to fly our country's flag. . . . Great tragedy has come to us, and we are meeting it with the best that is in our country, with courage and concern for others. Because this is America. This is who we are. This is what our enemies hate and have attacked. And this is why we will prevail."

GEORGE W. BUSH, U.S. president, September 15, 2001

41

42

together to pass bills aimed at keeping America safe and providing compensation to victims of the attacks. Not all Americans were included in this newfound sense of community, however. In some areas of the U.S., Muslims and people of Arabic descent faced verbal and physical abuse, despite the fact that most Muslims around the world had condemned the attacks.

Changes also took place in the U.S. government in the months after the attacks. The Office of Homeland Security was created to coordinate the efforts of the 40 agencies that deal with security in the U.S., and the Patriot Act was passed to make it easier for the FBI to tap phone conversations and monitor the Internet activity of suspected terrorists. Although the act was initially embraced as a necessary precaution, it soon aroused fears among

some politicians and citizens that Americans' civil liberties might be infringed upon. By 2007, the act remained a topic of hot debate.

Besides debating the government's response to the attack, politicians and citizens throughout America debated why the government had failed to prevent the attacks in the first place. In 2002, a Congressional committee known as the 9/11 Commission was formed to investigate the attacks. After reviewing more than 2.5 million pages of documents and interviewing more than 1,200 people, the commission released its final 567-page report in July 2004. In addition to analyzing events, the report also offered several recommendations to help prevent future attacks. One such recommendation was to raise security standards at U.S. borders, a recommendation that soon resulted

After September 11, National Guard troops patrolled U.S. airports, and passengers were prevented from packing items such as nail clippers in their carry-on luggage.

"*This is a moment when every difference between nations . . . [is] put to one side in one common endeavor. The world should stand together against this outrage. . . . Terrorism has taken on a new and frightening aspect. The people perpetrating it wear the ultimate badge of the fanatic: they are prepared to commit suicide in pursuit of their beliefs. Our beliefs are the very opposite of the fanatics. We believe in reason, democracy, and tolerance. . . . But the fanatics should know: we hold these beliefs every bit as strongly as they hold theirs.*"

TONY BLAIR, British prime minister, September 14, 2001

in a fierce debate between those calling for tightened border security and others calling for increased rights for immigrants. As of 2007, the controversy remained unresolved as members of Congress struggled to come to an agreement over an immigration reform bill.

Even while the U.S. government was working to establish new domestic policies to keep America safe, the country turned its sights in the war on terror to Iraq, long considered a rogue nation and suspected of working to develop weapons of mass destruction—including chemical, biological, and nuclear weapons—that the U.S. feared it would supply to terrorists. In March 2003, the U.S. invaded Iraq and within three weeks toppled Iraqi president Saddam Hussein's regime. In December, Hussein himself was captured. Yet hostilities didn't end, as guerrilla fighters, many of them Islamic extremists from Iraq and other countries, took aim at U.S. troops in a bloody battle that continued to plague the nation four years after the war's start.

Today, as U.S. troops remain engaged in the war on terror, Americans at home have not forgotten what sparked

"Those youths who did what they did and destroyed America with their airplanes did a good deed. They have moved the battle into the heart of America. America must know that the battle will not leave its land, God willing, until America leaves our land, until it stops supporting Israel, until it stops the blockade against Iraq. The Americans must know the storm of airplanes will not stop, God willing, and there are thousands of young people who are as keen about death as Americans are about life."

SULAIMAN ABU GHAITH, Al Qaeda spokesman, October 10, 2001

44

America's newfound sense of unity following the September 11 attacks proved to be short-lived. Within a year, both politicians and American citizens were again at odds, especially over the prospect of invading Iraq. Following the start of the Iraq War in March 2003, divisions became even deeper. In 2005, passionate calls from some Democrats to withdraw troops from Iraq were met with the equally passionate Republican response that doing so would make the still-tumultuous country a terrorist haven and invite more attacks on the U.S. The war caused global divisions as well, as countries that had pledged to support the U.S.-led war on terror questioned America's justifications for invading Iraq and refused to send troops.

When Saddam Hussein—who had ruled Iraq since 1979—was deposed in 2003, U.S. Marines pulled down a huge statue of the dictator that stood in the center of Baghdad.

With its 1,776 feet (541 m) paying tribute to the year of American independence, the Freedom Tower will stand as a new symbol of U.S. freedom and resilience.

that war. Each year on the anniversary of the attacks, memorial services are observed at the three attack sites, as well as in communities around the nation. At the Pentagon, a lasting memorial featuring a separate "memorial unit" for each of the 184 victims who died in the attack there is anticipated to be completed by 2008. By 2010, a giant skyscraper called the Freedom Tower will rise 1,776 feet (541 m) on the site of the former World Trade Center, and in Pennsylvania, a 2,200-acre (890 ha) memorial around the site of the crash of Flight 93 is projected to be completed by 2011. Even without these tangible tributes to the individuals who lost their lives on September 11, however, the events of that terrible day have been immortalized in the hearts of millions of Americans, who have vowed to never forget.

BIBLIOGRAPHY

Dwyer, Jim, and Kevin Flynn. *102 Minutes: The Untold Story of the Fight to Survive Inside the Twin Towers*. New York: Times Books, 2005.

Fink, Mitchell, and Lois Mathias. *Never Forget: An Oral History of September 11, 2001*. New York: HarperCollins, 2002.

Lalley, Patrick. *9.11.01: Terrorists Attack the U.S.* New York: Raintree Steck-Vaughn, 2002.

Levitas, Mitchel, ed. *A Nation Challenged*. New York: The New York Times, 2002.

Margulies, Phillip. *Al Qaeda: Osama bin Laden's Army of Terrorists*. New York: The Rosen Publishing Group, 2003.

National Commission on Terrorist Attacks Upon the United States. *The 9/11 Commission Report*. New York: W.W. Norton & Company, 2004.

Roleff, Tamara, ed. *The World Trade Center Attack*. San Diego: Greenhaven Press, 2003.

INDEX